THE JOY
OF SERVICE

THE JOY
OF SERVICE

Julian Hardyman

10 Publishing
a division of 10 ofthose.com

First published in Great Britain in 2016

British Library Cataloguing in Publication Data
A record for this book is available from the British Library

ISBN: 978-1-910587-96-6

Designed by Diane Warnes
Printed in Denmark by Nørhaven

10Publishing, a division of 10ofthose.com
Unit C, Tomlinson Road, Leyland, PR25 2DY, England
Email: info@10ofthose.com
Website: www.10ofthose.com

To John and Diana

CONTENTS

FOREWORD

Writing this little book has helped me retrieve some important memories; to refresh my sense of the privilege of my work as a pastor; to remind myself of the living reality of the powerful love which has entered my life in Christ; and above all to remind myself that serving Christ really is joyful. I have been a member of a number of churches but it is from my time as pastor of Eden Baptist Church that I have drawn most deeply in writing this book. The dear Eden folk have been patient with me and taught me a great deal. I owe them so much and love them more and more every passing year. I also want to mention my dear wife Debbie, and my children, Robin, Fiona and Kitty. Without Debbie's commitment I would have bailed out of ministry on several occasions and might never have got started in the first place! She has been with me through all the experiences described here and has been a great source of strength. My children have played their part too, both in patience and encouragement. The dedication is to my sister and brother-in-law, who have been kind and supportive in so many ways, including enabling me to find productive solitude in two very different places for writing and thinking and prayer. In addition, John has helped me by repeatedly pushing me towards an optimistic outlook more in keeping with our hope in Christ than my natural pessimism and anxiety. That has been a very great gift.

SERIES INTRODUCTION

The Hub Conference was launched in 2013 by the Fellowship of Independent Evangelical Churches (FIEC) as an annual conference to help men and women find clear routes into independent church ministry. For those 'just looking' as well as those 'just started', The Hub aims to be one means of support and advice on a possible journey through training and into gospel ministry.

Led by experienced gospel workers from the FIEC, and supported by leaders from colleges and courses, The Hub provides Bible ministry and a wide range of seminars on ministry-related issues.

It is out of this annual conference that this series of books was born. It occurred to the organising committee that these seminar topics could provide a helpful resource for anyone involved in gospel ministry, whether or not they attended The Hub or entered paid Christian ministry. In addition, the hope is that these books might also help pastors and leaders in discipling members of congregations for leadership and ministry.

Someone once described theological books as a *college of teachers committed to helping you do your best to handle the word of truth'.* We hope this series will play a small but significant part in that library of wisdom, at whatever stage you find yourself.

Though being a Christian and serving Christ will bring its challenges and at times be tough and dispiriting, it is nevertheless a joy! Too often the 'woe is me' spirit can overtake us and we lose sight of the joy that is involved in following Christ and belonging to him and having some small part to play in growing his Kingdom. This book by Julian Hardyman is a wonderful corrective to those tendencies and a realistic, practical, rooted and sensitive call to all gospel workers to find a renewed joy in serving our Master.

Trevor Archer and Dan Green
Series editors

INTRODUCTION

'I've been in pastoral ministry for over 30 years and it has been full of joy.'

The speaker was an experienced pastor called Robert. He'd been invited to our church to help us sort out a painful and intractable mess. Relationships were on edge. Wounds had been opened which were raw and painful. The leadership was divided. People weren't getting on. The future of the church was quite unclear. Confusion and suspicion hung in the air like a toxic fog.

Something was wrong. Perhaps more than one thing was wrong. And we'd all realised we weren't able to sort it out without outside help.

Three years before, I'd gone to my first elders' meeting. It felt quite unlike the relaxed, brotherly elders' meetings at the church where I had worked before. When I went home I said to my wife, 'Something's not right.' The three years that had followed some-times (not always) felt like walking in bare feet over broken glass.

So when I heard what Robert said about joy, my first thought was: 'Oh yeah?' But he was someone who commanded respect, so I shelved my scepticism to watch him at work and see what I could learn.

Now, in my early 50s, I can echo his words.

I truly can. 'I've been in pastoral ministry for over 20 years and it has been full of joy.' It really has. Greater joy than I think I imagined possible. Joy that is not a single point or moment but, as I recall it, is like a set of photos of a whole variety of holiday landscapes – hugely varied, all striking and beautiful. And those are the predominant memories of those years.

But as I have hinted, those are not the only memories. The story is more varied than that. My inner photo library also has pictures of some dark, sad and tense scenes. Scenes of broken objects and broken people, memories of emotional muscles aching because they had been pushed too far. Scenes of shame or pain, which I would rather not dwell on either because I sinned or because the ripples from someone else's shortcoming touched me. Times of deep weariness. Times when all I felt was emptiness. Times when I wished this was someone else's responsibility and even wished I wasn't.

So it has been a joy, but not an undiluted one. There's been both sin and pain, often connected. While I regret my sin, I have learned from it, from the way it has broken me and shown me more grace.

While I do wonder occasionally at just how hard things have been sometimes, I don't wish it had been easier or that we'd magically flown over those moments, like a migrating bird swerving upwards to avoid a forest fire. The fires have been the fire of growth – for me and for the church – and also of joy. And it has all been more than worth it.

I'd like to explain how – and to explain the connection between serving, ministry and joy.

Lord, it feels as though I've reached a point where I may have something to share. I pray for everyone who picks this little book up. Grant to them to hear your voice and sense your holy presence of magnetic love as they read. Amen.

MINISTRY AS SERVICE

When I was first asked to write this little book, I read the email too quickly and thought the title was supposed to be *The Joy of Ministry*. Some ideas started forming in my mind. Then I looked more closely and realised that the email said *The Joy of Service*.

The word *ministry* really means *service*, but in modern English the two are not often closely associated. That leads to all sorts of problems. Lots of us say 'ministry' and we mean 'profession'. Or, 'a set of Christian activities that I find fulfilling and which give me some sort of status, at least within the church. So it looks like a pretty good career choice'. That is not the biblical way and it leads us into problems. We need to glue the two words together again in our minds.

In the very early days of the church the apostles, the leaders Jesus had chosen, found they were getting overloaded. Wonderfully, lots of marginal and needy people had become Christians. Many of them were widows and had no easy way of providing for themselves. They depended on the church for meals on a daily basis. So the church set up a food bank. Management of this food bank rested on the shoulders of the apostles. It is rather lovely to realise how it shows us how much they cared about practical needs.

But, as so often, church growth brought new problems in its tailwind. The apostles weren't getting enough time for the critically important responsibilities entrusted specifically to *them*. So they called a church meeting, explained the issue and proposed a solution: find some reliable folk we can delegate the food bank to.

There is a lot that is interesting about this little episode. Let's look at the words they use. Here is what they say:

> 'It would not be right for us to neglect the ministry of the word of God in order *to wait on tables.* Brothers and sisters, choose seven men from among you who are known to be full of the Spirit and wisdom. We will turn this responsibility over to them and will give our attention *to prayer and the ministry of the word.*' Acts 6:2–4 (my italics)

They sum up the whole of their work as two things: prayer and the ministry of the word. The word they used for *ministry* in verse 4 is the same as the word for *waiting at tables* in verse 2. It is about *serving.* That is an easy word to understand but the pairing of it with 'the word' is unusual. The apostles were not trying to get out of the food bank – but they did have something that was more important for *them* to do.

So, what does serving 'the word' actually mean? In Acts 'the word' is not simply the whole of the Bible (which for them was the Old Testament). The word in Acts is the message of Jesus Christ, what we would call the gospel (as in verse 7 – 'So the word of God spread'). It is seen not simply as a set of ideas but a living dynamic force. It is the powerful speech of God unleashed in the world, which grows and spreads, bringing new life and unexpected hope wherever it goes. These days we talk about 'memes' – ideas which 'go viral' and spread rapidly. Acts portrays the word of God rather like a divine meme, going viral in the ancient world. But it is different because it spreads through divine power and the divine power comes from divine presence in the word – the Holy Spirit.

The apostles have a central role in this process because the word spreads through being communicated, being preached and explained. That is the work that must not be neglected, even for something as important as a daily food bank. And the picture they used to define their relationship with the work is *serving*.

Is that how you see Christian ministry? We could have chosen lots of other verses to demonstrate the same point. Paul, for example, repeatedly describes himself as a servant of Christ in his work, and therefore in the whole of his life. And servant meant slave.

Is that how you see your future as a youth pastor? Or a Bible translator? Or a pastor? You are a servant of the word of God. The word of God is God's presence in this world: it is God speaking about himself and his Son and his love. It is the most powerful meme in history. It has gone viral in a way nothing else, not even human sin, has done. And your relationship to it is defined by the word 'service': you are its servant.

There is a wonderful positive side to this, mind you. I have a friend who was the pastor of the same church for 45 years. When he started there were around 40 members. When he retired in 2015 there were 750 adults and children in church every Sunday morning. The secret?

It is all in Acts 6. My friend basically did three things very well (and I mean very well): prayer, preaching and finding others to share the work of love in the church.

I asked him once what it had been like. He said it had felt like being on a huge ocean-going liner. He felt he was no more than the man on the bridge who steered it a bit either way but had nothing to do with the power of the ship's engines. All the momentum, all the stability, all the safety for the passengers and crew, all the wonderful sights along the way, came from the word of God, an unstoppable power that he saw at work and marvelled at. I suspect that he saw the growth he did because he was a servant of the word, and not the other way round. It is hard to imagine a greater privilege for a life's work than seeing broken lives healed; people, who no one would ever have imagined in church, raising their arms in worship week by week and lives burdened by care and consumption released into rest in Christ.

Let me ask you again, is that how you see yourself in ministry? If you are like me you need to think about that rather carefully and pray it through. Here is how I did that:

> *Lord, I'm a mystery to myself and what I do see is very mixed. I am not sure that ministry has always meant service for me. In fact, I am sure it's often meant something else. I find it hard to admit it to myself, let alone to you and the folk who may read this, but quite a lot of the time, ministry has meant serving self. I have used it to try to feel good about myself. I have done it and described it in ways that are carefully angled to make myself look good. I have made the word my servant rather than the other way round. You can see deeper than I can into the cavern of my inner life: I rather shudder to think what you can see. But I cling to your grace: and I find a safe place in the forgiveness which is the heart of the message of the word. And I think of the new creation which the word has germinated in my soul. And I pledge myself again to serving the word, not making it serve me. And I find rest. Amen.*

MINISTRY AND SACRIFICE

We've seen that ministry – working as a pastor or missionary or youth worker or whatever – is a life of serving the word of God, the dynamic force which is the centre of God's plan for our tortured and blind world. Where does the momentum of that word come from? The answer is Jesus Christ, the word of God (John 1:1,14) – specifically the life, death and resurrection of Christ, and even more specifically the cross where he died for us and all our moral darkness. The cross, which looked so much like a dead end, a waste tip for human hope, in fact unleashed an 'unsurpassable momentum of the glory of divine love',[1] through the resurrection.

This momentum meets us in the life of the church: we don't just hear about self-giving love when we go to church or speak with other Christians. We meet it. It meets us, in wave after wave of living encounters with a living Christ. And it determines its own pattern for us to experience it:

> 'And [Jesus] said, "The Son of Man must suffer many things and be rejected by the elders, the chief priests and the teachers of the law, and he must be killed and on the third day be raised to life."

Then he said to them all: "Whoever wants to be my disciple must deny themselves and take up their cross daily and follow me. For whoever wants to save their life will lose it, but whoever loses their life for me will save it. What good is it for someone to gain the whole world, and yet lose or forfeit their very self? Whoever is ashamed of me and my words, the Son of Man will be ashamed of them when he comes in his glory and in the glory of the Father and of the holy angels."

"Truly I tell you, some who are standing here will not taste death before they see the kingdom of God."' Luke 9:22–27

Here we are seeing the pattern for anyone who wants to follow Jesus. This is not just for those 'in ministry' but any potential disciple. So of course it includes those in ministry or considering ministry.

The pattern is set by the cross: no one could ever say Jesus isn't clear about that. It is a lifelong pattern of relinquishing control and direction over my own life and giving it over to Him, whatever the cost. And there will be a cost: we see that in the picture of picking up a cross every day. I used to wonder how that worked: a cross is a means of execution, so if I pick it up, I'm heading towards death – can I do that every day?

I have learned that my desire to be in control won't go away. My desires for goals which aren't God's will for me keep reappearing. So I have to expect to die a new mini-death every day, often many mini-deaths every day.

And I don't like it! I like being in charge. I am pretty confident about what will make me most happy and I feel good when I can bend all my energies to getting it. That is the way of our whole culture, devoted to self-fulfilment, which I am part of.

Frankly – the cross is great if it makes me feel OK about my failures and generates a passcode to get me into heaven. But the cross as a pattern of living – I could do without it. But actually I can't do without it – either in ministry or in life. There is no alternative pattern for either – nor could we expect there to be if we are to resemble a crucified saviour. For we live out the message and become living embodiments of it.

Let's bring that down to earth and apply it to ministry. Ministry means carrying a cross. It means for just about everyone who reads this book that you will earn less money and live in a smaller house or flat than if you had chosen another way to spend your working life. As you get older those differentials will grow: the kinds of holidays you have may well look very different. You will possibly use a different supermarket. You will change your car less often and have a smaller or older model than your brother.

It means less choice in how you spend your time than most of your friends have. We had some friends who told one of my children that they were going away for the weekend. Her response (aged perhaps six or seven) was wide-eyed: 'Mummy, do people *go away* for *weekends*?'

There are times when it is impossible not to work four or five evenings in a particular week. Many of my meetings are in the evenings because the others involved work during the day: I am often tired by the evening. It takes a lot out of me to summon the will not just to go to the meeting, but to lead it in a way which is wise and properly attentive to others.

Ministry families must follow this pathway together. It is hard for the children who get little or no choice about it, but that is the biblical way. It seems strange to our highly individualised Western culture but it is the biblical way. My father had lifelong double vision. His parents were missionaries in Madagascar so he was unable to have the corrective surgery he needed on his eyes when he was young.

Wives and husbands have more choice; if your wife or husband isn't willing to embrace the hard sides of ministry, you should stay away from it. They also have to expect to exercise it, not just once but repeatedly.

Several of my colleagues, two of them with small children, work til 9 or 10pm on Sundays in term time.

It's a really important part of our student ministry. It is also the last time most people want to be working. And it is very much the last time any of their spouses want them to be working: those who minister and their families both have to pick up a cross every Sunday at 5:30pm when they head out for four hours, leaving the others at home.

Ministry means working very hard. That was Paul's way and it is ours: labouring, striving, giving ourselves again and again to demanding and repetitive tasks. Some of the time it will be hard work which you don't much care for. In spite of the Acts 6 principle, many folk in ministry end up doing lots of things that aren't prayer and preaching, some of it menial and tedious.

Ministry means walking towards other people's pain.[2] Who wants to do that? If you are in ministry what *you* want is irrelevant: you do it, as part of picking up your cross. At times ministry means suffering injustice and not retaliating and suffering shame and not seeking vindication. That is not theoretical: I can think of two or three dear friends who have chosen not to seek the kind of personal vindication which natural justice would require but have chosen a higher path – silence.

I have to remind myself of two things: first there is only one way of following Jesus: the Calvary Road. No cross, no Christian discipleship. For me to want the benefits of the cross without its demands is not just rude, it's impossible. Not an option. Ministry without a cross is not ministry.

And there is a second thing. Another translation of Luke 9:24, from the NLT, helps me understand it: 'If you try to hang on to your life, you will lose it.'

Aim for self-fulfilment and I'll not find myself turning into the shiniest, most impressive version of myself that I can be, but rusting like a piece of iron in the rain. Aim for Jesus AND control of my own life, and I'll find my self getting progressively smaller, uglier, and nastier, shrivelling and rotting away from the inside like an apple that has fallen off the tree and lies on the ground uneaten.

But taking up my cross does the opposite. The surprising paradox is that as I forget myself because I am looking so much at the cross, I find myself, as I was always meant to be. As I give of myself in the power of the Spirit, I find that my inner life is more and more Christ-shaped and I am becoming the best possible version of myself. As I deny myself, I am taking bigger and bigger steps along a road to the dazzling moment when the glory of God takes over the universe – and I will be on the right side of it. Even now it means a view like no other.

> 'Truly I tell you, some who are standing here will not taste death before they see the kingdom of God.' Luke 9:27

Sacrifice in ministry gives us the most beautiful sight in the world: Jesus recreating broken human lives.

In the here and now, in a world that has no true transformative power, we get to see supernatural love at work, through our service of other people. It is hard but it is worth it. I truly believe that – because I have experienced it so consistently. The same is true for many of my friends who are also in ministry. There is no sight comparable and it makes everything worthwhile.

And my father, although he was never able to drive a car, had to read by ignoring the second set of letters he always saw, and was comically inept at ball games, never complained about the double vision that resulted from his parents being missionaries. On the contrary, he saw that upbringing as the greatest of privileges, with the double vision an unfortunate but necessary and bearable consequence of that privilege.

Lord, you chose the cross – but I hate it. Oh, I love the forgiveness it brings: what a relief. And nothing feels more wonderful than being loved unconditionally. But self-denial? If I am honest, no thanks. Why can't I do ministry my way? Why does it have to be this way? Is it because it is your way? I look at the cross again and I am so ashamed of my resistance. That sight, the immortal dying, your frail body, your vulnerable soul – you melt my heart again. How can it be any other way? How else can I have a part in the great momentum of love? Take me over again. Grant me help not to hang onto my life but to hang on to you. Amen.

MINISTRY AND SUFFERING

We have been thinking about cross-bearing as integral and non-negotiable for Christian ministry and indeed discipleship. You can no more be a Christian or a pastor without picking up your cross than you can play the piano without practising.

I am afraid we need to take this further! The pattern of cross-shaped lives for those in Christian ministry is fleshed out in 2 Corinthians in Paul's own life.

A few years ago I began meeting a student to share our lives, read the Bible together and pray. We agreed to study 2 Corinthians. I can't remember who suggested it, but I do remember vividly that we began by reading the first half of chapter one out loud. And I started crying. It was one of the more embarrassing moments of my life. He rather charmingly said: 'Don't worry, your secret is safe with me!' as I explained that Paul's description of suffering in ministry seemed to reflect some of my own experience, at least as I saw it.

> '**We do not want you to be uninformed, brothers and sisters, about the troubles we experienced in the province of Asia. We were under great pressure, far beyond our ability to endure, so that we despaired of life itself. Indeed, we felt we had received the sentence of death.**' 2 Corinthians 1:8–9

Paul reports 'troubles in the province of Asia', so toxic that the pressure was beyond his 'ability to endure'. He reached the point of thinking death was inevitable.

That is what it feels like at times in ministry. The pressure feels impossible. It may be the unreasonably high expectations of others or ourselves. It may be the entirely reasonable expectations that we or others have for our work. It may be physical or mental illness. It may be all manner of internal difficulties in church. It may be a cupboard full of plates that all seem to need spinning simultaneously. Whatever the reason we feel overwhelmed, like a person out at sea who thinks the next wave may mean death. That really is how it feels at times!

I have often felt like that. I used to think that I might grow out of it as I got a bit more experienced and it is true that I have developed a kind of professional confidence in my 'technical' competence at some aspects of the work that means that I can relax a bit more than I used to.

But I have not grown out of the stomach-churning sense on a Sunday morning that my preparation even at its best is going to produce a sermon that sounds about as interesting to my listeners as the Latvian telephone directory.

I still frequently sit down for that pre-service prayer time and feel that if everyone knew how empty and conflicted I am inside, they'd march me off to the crèche so I could start all over again. I come back from a summer holiday and genuinely wonder how on earth I will find the energy that the different bits of my job scream for if they are to be done even half-effectively. And I still find myself seeing folk with different problems and thinking I just don't know what to say or even how to share their pain.

But there is nothing inherently unbiblical about that. In fact, I want to suggest that we must, we absolutely must, expect our own version of Paul's experience of over-pressure. Because that is the way God helps us help others.

I remember interviewing someone for a senior ministry position (not at my church). He had many strengths and was suitable in many ways. I felt prompted to take a line of questioning we had not planned. 'Can you tell us how you have suffered?' I asked. He smiled. There had been some difficulties but much of his life had been relatively easy. Somehow that showed. It wasn't his fault and things may have been very different since then.

Paul's experience of pressure enabled him to help others under pressure.

> 'Praise be to the God and Father of our Lord
> Jesus Christ, the Father of compassion and the
> God of all comfort, who comforts us in all our

troubles, so that we can comfort those in any trouble with the comfort we ourselves receive from God. For just as we share abundantly in the sufferings of Christ, so also our comfort abounds through Christ. If we are distressed, it is for your comfort and salvation; if we are comforted, it is for your comfort, which produces in you patient endurance of the same sufferings we suffer. And our hope for you is firm, because we know that just as you share in our sufferings, so also you share in our comfort.' 2 Corinthians 1:3–7

Paul's experience of being so far out of his comfort zone he had forgotten what it looked like was central to his ability to care for others. In that highly uncomfortable zone, he had found more of the extraordinary tenderness of Christ which meets us at our precise point of need and injects a new capacity to endure.

I think of someone I know in ministry who has suffered repeated bouts of ill health. It's been frightening for her at times and she has never tried to fake a peace about it that she did not know. But the repeated cycles of illness have drawn her closer to Christ. They have given her a deeper empathy for others and somehow comfort she has received has a natural overflow into the lives of fellow sufferers. It is hard for me to be objective about this but I think the same has been true for me. My struggles with anxiety and depression have been pretty gruesome at times, but I think they have helped me help others in a way that would not have been possible otherwise.

So, my ministry friend: let God work and he will break you – and then make you into someone he can use to help others.

Lord, I know a bit of this. Those early years at Eden were pretty extreme. I didn't always handle them well either, so there was sin to confess as well as pain to endure. And the breakdowns Debbie and I had took us both right to the edge: sometimes I did wonder if I'd have to make an exit, stage left. But in your grace you got us through them. And I think I can help people a bit better than I would have been able to without them. Thank you. But now I find myself thinking it's all in the past: I've learned those lessons. But that can't be right, can it Lord? If I stop running, I lose speed and strength. I can't rely on the fitness I had last autumn: I need fitness now. So if you need to break me all over again, perhaps even more painfully, I want to say 'do it', but I find it hard to. But what else can I say to you who do all things well? Amen.

MINISTRY AND POWER

We haven't quite finished with suffering and 2 Corinthians. Can you cope with a bit more? I hope so because this takes us deeper into the three-way connection between ministry, suffering and joy.

Let's start here: Do you ever lick your ministry wounds and count them? I know I do. There are healthy ways of doing that and unhealthy ways. In chapter eleven Paul looks back over his life in ministry in a healthy way, healthy because the tone is not self-pity but gratitude to Christ.

> 'Five different times the Jewish leaders gave me thirty-nine lashes. Three times I was beaten with rods. Once I was stoned. Three times I was shipwrecked. Once I spent a whole night and a day adrift at sea. I have traveled on many long journeys. I have faced danger from rivers and from robbers. I have faced danger from my own people, the Jews, as well as from the Gentiles. I have faced danger in the cities, in the deserts, and on the seas. And I have faced danger from men who claim to be believers but are not. I have worked hard and long, enduring many sleepless nights. I have been hungry and thirsty and have often gone without food. I have shivered in the cold, without enough clothing to keep me warm.

> Then, besides all this, I have the daily burden of my concern for all the churches. Who is weak without my feeling that weakness? Who is led astray, and I do not burn with anger?'
> 2 Corinthians 11:24–29 (NLT)

What a catalogue! Then he goes on to speak of a particular spike of pain. He calls it a 'thorn in my flesh' (2 Cor. 12:7), something that God allowed Satan to use to 'torment me'. That is strong language: when I get a thorn stuck in my skin it's usually just a little prick, though sometimes it lasts and niggles. But Paul's thorn tormented him. Sometimes when I haul myself into our garden for an hour's inept hacking, I end up with a little thorn from a rose bush in my finger (a raspberry thorn is even smaller). it's tiny but it really hurts. Paul's thorn was agony, like walking with a spike through his foot. Or a nail... And it wouldn't go away. Even though it made him weak. Even though it seemed to make ministry harder. And even though he asked God three times to take it away. It just kept on tormenting. What God *did* give him, in the voice of Jesus himself, was an explanation:

> 'My grace is sufficient for you, for my power is made perfect in weakness.' 2 Corinthians 12:9

The powerful dynamic of the word, that great supernatural momentum released through the cross and resurrection, the energy of the gospel viral meme which those in ministry transmit every time they give a short Bible thought – all are strangely completed and perfected through the weakness of those doing ministry. And that is the point of the letter: a crucified saviour who willingly embraces weakness in the incarnation and on the cross can only be properly passed on by servants who willingly accept weakness and vulnerability.

How does this work in practice? Lots of hardship in Christian ministry just happens to us. We get ill. Family members get ill. Fellow staff members or volunteers get ill and their responsibilities fall on us. Many of us find we have unwanted thorns in the flesh of many different kinds which torment us. I think of friends with brain tumours, chronic pain, chronic fatigue, repeated bouts of pneumonia, colostomy bags, unpleasant and incurable skin conditions, a psychiatric text book of mental illnesses in their own lives and families. A ministry job does not immunise us against all the common hardships of life – and it may be that God allows Satan to intensify or even multiply them against those in ministry: Satan would certainly like that.

And all of it is part of God's plan to make his power perfect in weakness. Every single hard thing that has burst into your life or crept up behind you and grabbed you; every single physical pain; every bit of heartache; every infection; every experience of being totally overwhelmed – all of it, without exception is part of God's plan to make Christ all the more real, attractive and persuasive to others (and to you).

And so Paul's response is not bravado or a sort of twisted spiritual masochism. it is entirely rational. And it can be our response too:

> 'Therefore I will boast all the more gladly about my weaknesses, so that Christ's power may rest on me. That is why, for Christ's sake, I delight in weaknesses, in insults, in hardships, in persecutions, in difficulties. For when I am weak, then I am strong.' 1 Corinthians 12:9–10

Joy in suffering and joy because of suffering. Because it means more supernatural power in my life, more of the only strength that really counts; more impact for the gospel in my life and other people's lives too. Because God comes to broken people:

> 'For this is what the high and exalted One says –
>   he who lives for ever, whose name is holy:
> "I live in a high and holy place,
>   but also with the one who is contrite and lowly in spirit,
> to revive the spirit of the lowly
>   and to revive the heart of the contrite."'
> Isaiah 57:15

A friend of mine explained it like this:

> '"Contrite" means crushed, pulverised, shattered. This word is used elsewhere in the Old Testament for dust as something ground down to bits. Inevitably, if God has a purpose of grace and glory for you, you will be crushed. A. W. Tozer said it well: "It is doubtful whether God can bless a man greatly until He has hurt him deeply." One pathway to blessing that we would never choose – so God chooses it for us – is to suffer.'[3]

When I read that, I thought of a friend of mine who has lost two children and has had a very hard time in Christian ministry. With this in mind, I wrote to him after he had preached powerfully while being really quite unwell:

> 'In his strange, loving wisdom, God has crushed you repeatedly and hurt you deeply. You have responded with submission and trust. The result is a preacher and leader of quite unusual humility, authority, and maturity from whom gospel power and wisdom ooze out like rivers of gold. As a preacher you now have an unusual authority and wisdom which is marked and powerful – the sort of thing that cannot be taught or contrived but is given by the Holy Spirit. And you were arising from your sick bed last night!

Tough though your journey has been, even simply to observe at times, the result now is truly inspirational: you are a very special gift as friend, pastor and national leader. All the way through He has a "purpose of grace and glory for you" which is now more and more evident. Praise God!'

He wrote back:

'This email was lovely to receive but a little more difficult to know how to respond to! Inevitably I feel the reality falls short of much of what you perceive but I am aware of being very shaped both by the pain the Lord has permitted in my life and the grace he has supplied in responding to it. It is a deep encouragement to know that someone who knows me as well as you do can see the fruit of it in my life and I long that it should be more and more so.'

He went on to speak of how some of the difficult things that have happened to me in ministry have had an impact on me. I suppose I dimly sense that myself: church conflicts, excruciating church meetings, tense and fractured elders' meetings, church division about me in the most personal of ways, four years of preaching with a view pretty well every Sunday and wondering if I would have a job at the end of it, a boss who behaved increasingly oddly and then defected from both his family and his ministry, an (admittedly self-imposed) crushing sense of needing to be better than I knew I was or could be at preaching, one major breakdown and years of living on the edge of anxiety and depression, serious mental illness in the family and some extremely difficult relationships.

I am a bit embarrassed listing these as I have done, for fear of it seeming like a rather over-dramatic bid for pity. But the list does describe, I think without exaggeration, a part of my experiences of ministry in Cambridge (almost all of it some years past, much of it many years ago in the gruelling early period).

And I am glad it all happened. Every single bit. Except for the bits where I sinned, though they have their own part in God's unfolding plan to make me relatively more mature than could have happened any other way. And that maturity has largely been the embrace of weakness as an operating principle for my life and ministry.

I have an image for this which I love. It comes from the rarefied world of Japanese porcelain and is called a *kintsugi*. It starts as a porcelain bowl, perfectly round, made of thin delicate china, with exquisite patterns and painting under the glaze. The potter then breaks it. She doesn't pulverise it into tiny dust. But it is broken into pieces. This is all quite deliberate. Next, she prepares a gold ceramic cement. With the cement she glues the pieces back together. The result is far more beautiful than the first bowl.

That is a picture of the hand of God in the suffering of his servants – providing they are ready to submit to it.

> *Lord, I've always needed you to break me and I still do. So you did break me and you keep breaking. Repeatedly. How rough the blows that break feel at the time. But how kind they turn out to be! I almost always see them as one-way gates into gloom but so many have turned out to be doors into rose gardens and alpine meadows. You have so consistently shown that you knew best. So often, I thought I did but I was wrong. Thank you. Amen.*

MINISTRY AND PERSECUTION

I started paid ministry as Church Manager and Pastoral Assistant. It was a bit of a mouthful but it more or less described what I did. The next Christmas I went to Debbie's work Christmas party. The room was full of dentists having a jolly time talking about extractions that had gone wrong, or whatever dentists talk about at parties. A senior lady approached me. She was the wife of one of the consultants who were Debbie's joint bosses. This is how the conversation went:

- And *who* are you?
- I am Deborah's husband.
- And *who* is Deborah?
- One of your husband's juniors.
- And what do *you* do?
- I am a Church Manager and Pastoral Assistant.
- Do they *pay* people to do that sort of thing?

I felt rather as though I had met Lady Bracknell from Oscar Wilde's play, *The Importance of Being Earnest*. I thought she might well next declaim 'A *handbag*?' It was clear that working for a church did not impress her: 'A *pastor*?' she might have said.

We went to another party a little while afterwards at the house of one of our neighbours. This one was less multi-generational: everyone else there seemed to be in their 20s like us and it had a good buzz about it. No sign of any Lady Bracknells. That's a relief.

I got talking with a fellow guest: I asked him about himself and his work for a while. Then he asked me what I did. 'I work for a church.' Without another word, he turned away and started a conversation with someone else. I did the same: I asked this second guest about himself and his work for a while. Then he asked me what I did. 'I work for a church.' Without another word, he turned away and started a conversation with someone else. I did the same. I asked her about herself and her work for a while. Then she asked me what I did. 'I work for a church.' Without another word, she turned away and started a conversation with someone else. At this point I got a little sense of the high social standing of church workers in that part of Nottingham.

A few years ago I was out on the street outside our church building in Cambridge. It is pedestrianised. I was there inviting people to come in for a cup of coffee. I approached one man with a flyer. He realised I was connected with the church and his expression turned sour. 'Hypocrites. Abusers. Nothing but trouble,' is a short summary of what he said. What took me aback was the venom of his tone.

A part of the life of the Christian disciple in ministry (or out of it) is to experience negative reactions and treatment from people outside the church (and sometimes inside too). Jesus warns us to expect it (John 15:18–19).

The word 'persecution' describes the more extreme forms of this. One minister I know came from a Jewish family. They cut him off when he became a Christian. I met a Christian worker called John from East Africa. He had been tortured and left for dead by a gang. A ministry friend of his had to photograph his torture wounds to provide the evidence needed for asylum in Canada. The photographer still suffers from post-traumatic stress disorder.

In Acts 5, the apostles are arrested by the Jewish religious authorities in Jerusalem. They are put in jail. No jails, outside Scandinavia, are nice: no jails anywhere in the first century were the sort of places you would want to spend a second of your time.

Miraculously, they escape – and go back to what they were doing before – public communication of the word of Christ, all over again. They are called in again. This time the authorities decide to take things more gently so they let them go with a warning not to preach any more. Oh, and with a flogging too. A flogging.

I have never been flogged and I never want to be. If I were flogged I imagine I would feel pretty sorry for myself. I suppose the flogging was a way of saying: we have the power over you to do this – and worse if you keep on with your pesky preaching. What did they do?

> 'The apostles left the Sanhedrin, rejoicing because they had been counted worthy of suffering disgrace for the Name.' Acts 5:41

You did not misread that. They had been publicly shamed, imprisoned, forbidden to preach, and then beaten. And they went home dancing on air (albeit a bit gingerly, perhaps). The Name is the Name of Jesus, or more fully, the Lord Jesus Christ. They only spoke in his Name: all they had to offer was through his Name. His Name was a badge, a summary, a sign, even a kind of representation of his personal presence and power in their lives and words. His Name was the umbrella term for the unstoppable momentum of divine love which has been unleashed at the cross.

Being associated with his Name was the highest privilege they could imagine, like a stateless refugee who becomes a citizen of a civilised country and can hardly believe the privilege of being able to call themselves a Swedish or Canadian citizen. But the highest privilege of all was to suffer for the Name – and notice the kind of suffering: disgrace.

Physical suffering is horrible. But disgrace and shame can be very hard to bear. I tasted a little of that when those three party-goers shunned me one after the other. So why should they rejoice in the disgrace? Because it is a privilege to be associated with Jesus. And, more deeply, because he himself experienced shame and disgrace. That was what made the cross so terrible: the shame of it. So for us to be disgraced is to get closer to Jesus than perhaps we can any other way. The author of Hebrews puts it like this, using picture language for a movement we can all make:

> **'Jesus also suffered outside the city gate to make the people holy through his own blood. Let us, then, go to him outside the camp, bearing the disgrace he bore. For here we do not have an enduring city, but we are looking for the city that is to come.' Hebrews 13:12–14**

Opposition from our society and culture is inevitable but it generates its own rarified and special joy, and its own ultimate prize.

What does that look like in practice? It shapes our reaction to the scorn for Christian faith, the Christian church and Christian work that is expressed so often in the media or in drama and soap opera. Sometimes it is open contempt. More often for me, it is when friends are polite about my work and faith but clearly see it as little more than believing that there are fairies at the bottom of my garden and building a career on that delusion. This is our go-to text when we are ostracised, excluded, even victimised and abused: our response to all these things is modelled by the apostles as they see it as high privilege and a confirmation of their relationship with Jesus. And like them it propels us on in serving the word:

> 'Day after day, in the temple courts and from house to house, they never stopped teaching and proclaiming the good news that Jesus is the Messiah.' Acts 5:42

Either you have experienced shame, or you will. Some sort of highly negative reaction will come your way in your life in Christian ministry. Will you run away from it? Will you react with anger, a desire to get even or to protect your rights? Or will you rejoice at the sheer privilege because the hard words or deeds show that you are in union with Christ? It is hard, isn't it? Here's how I found I needed to pray about this:

Lord, I really struggle with this. I hate my faith being scorned on TV. I find it really hard that all sorts of bits of the gospel sound so politically incorrect. I know that I sometimes get laughed at or patronised for being a Christian. It feels so awful that people think Christian belief is risible or even toxic. None of it seems remotely joyful to me most of the time. I guess I want to be liked and accepted and respected. I hate the shame and I hate the disgrace. Right at the beginning of my Christian life I remember being mocked and even threatened at school. Lord, all I can say is that my responses are a long way from the example the apostles gave and I usually run away from the place of disgrace where you live. It feels like all I can do is ask for your help and offer you my determination in advance not to run away from potential opposition and to rejoice when (and if) it comes. Amen.

MINISTRY AND RESPONSIBILITY

A friend of mine who served a church for decades really loved his people. You could tell. One long-term member said, 'He talks about the church like a father glowing with joy at a child who has just won a place at a top university.' That summed it up nicely.

The lovely thing was that they loved him too. Not because he could do everything, or got everything right all the time: he didn't. His weak points were obvious enough (especially to him), and he had his sins (just as they did). But they knew that he loved them and they drew from his God-centred preaching and they were happy to follow his lead, though not blindly. It was a happy church.

This sort of pattern underlies the way the writer to the Hebrews speaks about church:

> **'Have confidence in your leaders and submit to their authority, because they keep watch over you as those who must give an account. Do this so that their work will be a joy, not a burden, for that would be of no benefit to you.' Hebrews 13:17**

We are accountable not only for ourselves and our faithful use of our gifts but for the people we serve.

Ministry often means some sort of authority, but it is a delegated authority from Christ himself. It is the authority my daughter gives me for her hamster when she goes away: 'You better look after it properly or else, Dad!' I suspect that the hamster analogy has its limits and my apologies to any Eden members who read this.

There are two sides to what the Hebrews writer is saying. From the minister's side it means self-denial and commitment. Again we come back to the joy of ministry as the joy of service. Taking on responsibility for a group of people is a sober thing to do.

And if we see them as our little empire, our source of self-esteem, the place where we get to feel good about ourselves, it all goes sour very quickly. I remember being shocked by hearing a very senior minister say dismissively that he would have left years before if it hadn't been for the students in his church. Or hearing another senior minister being described as strutting around after a service.

It means that sometimes we have to say tough and challenging things, in sermons (which is hard enough) but also face to face (much harder). That is our responsibility. Not for nothing does Paul use the verbs 'rebuke' and 'correct' in 2 Timothy 3:16, when he describes the quality and purpose of Scripture.

A wise people expect to be rebuked and corrected – in love and in due proportion and of course in the humility of a fellow sinner with all sorts of blind spots of his own. A less wise group may need to learn that that is what they pay the minister for!

Sometimes there is relational tension and even breakdown. That was why Paul needed to write 2 Corinthians. And at times I have had to call folk or meet them to apologise because I have been abrasive or thoughtless or neglectful.

But the biblical pattern is that we grow together as a family. The church watches us growing – Paul says to young Timothy:

> 'Be diligent in these matters; give yourself wholly to them, so that everyone may see your progress.' 1 Timothy 4:15

He expects that Timothy will be growing, but Timothy needs to be really hard-working and exacting for that to happen and, if he is, then people will see that he is maturing in faith and love and ministry. And we serve the church by praying and sharing God's word with them, doing our bit in the releasing the energy of Bible text after Bible text in their lives.

And we see their progress. It is delightful! I can think of people who have grown a great deal over 20 years, even though they were already mature Christians and over 70 years old at the start! I can think of others who seemed quite loose in their commitment and tentative (or even conflicted) in their faith, who have grown hugely. I can think of young people whose childhood enthusiasm for the fun and buzz of church, with its childlike acceptance of Jesus as a great friend, has transmuted into the deep commitment of young adults, totally committed to Jesus and the gospel, whatever the implications for their lives. And it doesn't get better than that!

At its best, ministry leaders and the people they serve work together so that the leaders work effectively and the people grow through their work. There is great joy for the leaders in seeing that. The fact that Paul has to tell people to make this happen shows that it is not automatic and sometimes it is difficult. But he expects it to work. He expects it to produce growth and joy of the kind John writes about when he says:

> 'I have no greater joy than to hear that my children are walking in the truth.' 3 John 4

Paul models a way of praying that is almost always mixed with thanksgiving. You find it in the first chapters of Colossians and Philippians and 2 Corinthians: he explodes with thanksgiving when he prays for them, even when there are substantial concerns about the life of the churches he is praying for. Perhaps most lovely of all is the brief summary in 1 Thessalonians 3:9:

'How can we thank God enough for you in return for all the joy we have in the presence of our God because of you?'

Here we have a snapshot of Paul's life of prayer. He is in the presence of God: he has drawn near by faith and is enjoying the love of Father, Son and Spirit. His thoughts turn to the Christians in Thessalonica and his heart fills with joy: he thinks about their 'work produced by faith, your labour prompted by love, and your endurance inspired by hope in our Lord Jesus Christ' (1 Thes. 1:3). And he is deeply moved with joy and thanksgiving. So much so that he even gives thanks for the thanks and is joyful at the joy.

If prayer for people is only concerned about their deficiencies and how God can correct them, it is not biblically balanced and it is not joyful! I have realised that I quite often see what could improve and focus on that. And I miss what God has already done and is currently doing in our church and in individual people's lives.

I suffer a bit from what psychologists call 'Other orientated perfectionism'. That means setting impossibly high standards for others and feeling critical and disappointed when I perceive that they have failed to meet them. It is not a good outlook. But it can be corrected! We can all learn to pray Paul's way, looking attentively at what God has done and is doing.

Rather than think about church folk for what they aren't, I lead myself into these sorts of thoughts: it is simply a miracle of divine grace that people are part of church at all. I look out on a Sunday morning and silently give thanks for another week in which God has preserved the spiritual momentum of these dear Christians. I go through the members' list and find myself marvelling at the hard work, the commitment, the zeal, the energy, the patience, the godliness, the self-denial that the photographs represent. It is immensely joyful.

Lord, thank you for Eden, this church family that I can be a part of and help to lead. I thank you that spiritually it is like a garden, with oaks of righteousness, and vines hung with clusters of grapes, a sea of spring flowers in a desert. Thank you for the real commitment I see. Thank you for the courage of people's commitment to you and your paths for human life. Thank you for the rebuilding of the community, through the power of the word, after the earthquakes of the late 1990s. Thank you that you are still at work in us and have plans for our future. Amen.

MINISTRY AND PRAYER

When the apostles realised that they were being stretched too thinly, they explained what the core tasks of their work were. Here is a reminder of what they said:

> '"We will turn this responsibility over to them and will give our attention to prayer and the ministry of the word."' Acts 6:3–4

Compared to the way many people in ministry find their work being shaped, there are two surprises here. The first is that it is not just preaching (the ministry of the word) but that prayer is put on the same level of importance. The second is that prayer is listed first.

I have tried to re-shape how I spend my time accordingly. It can be hard, with so many demands on my time. But this is the New Testament pattern. We see it in Paul's record of his prayers: so many of his letters include parts which are not just about prayer, they are about his prayers – and even summarise the wording of his prayers.

Prayer is, simply, central, integral and foundational to the work of ministry. Trying to do ministry without praying is like trying to play the trumpet without breathing or trying to sail a boat when there is no wind. Plenty of us try, though.

Prayer is not only vital, it is also hard work. That is very clear from Paul's description of one of his colleagues in Colossians 4:12:

> 'Epaphras, who is one of you and a servant of Christ Jesus, sends greetings. He is always wrestling in prayer for you, that you may stand firm in all the will of God, mature and fully assured.'

'Wrestling in prayer' conjures up the picture of a man striving with all his might and main to move a large rock. Or a rugby player in the scrum straining every sinew to rip the ball from his opponent. Let's imagine Epaphras praying for the Colossians. His brow is furrowed, his face screwed up, the tension goes all the way through his body. But the real battle is going on in his heart as he brings them and their needs to God again and again.

Perhaps words from Isaiah 62:6–7 inspire him:

> 'You who call on the LORD,
>   give yourselves no rest,
>   and give him no rest till he establishes Jerusalem
>   and makes her the praise of the earth.'

He thinks of individual friends at Colossae: he knows some of them are quite spiritually fragile. Some find the boundaries of Christ's commands hard to live within. Some are just young Christians, full of enthusiasm, but needing to work out their faith steadily over time and to find how the grace of God touches every part of their lives. Some don't have a consistent assurance that God's love will never let them go: it is there at times, but it flickers and sometimes is hardly more than a spark.

And so he brings them to God again and again. He picks on specific promises in God's word and urges God to make them real in the lives of these friends. He prays for a bit, feels worn out, but has no sense that it is right to stop, so he reads a bit of the word, gets new energy and is off again, pressing God to work. After a while he really is tired. The mental concentration is exhausting and it is emotionally pretty draining too as praying like this takes a lot out of him. So he gets on with some household responsibilities. But the next day he has no sense that it is right to stop praying for those folk in Colossae, so he starts again, working his way through the mental lists.

That is one part of the work of prayer in ministry: intercession for people. It means sacrifice. I give up other things in order to pray, whether on my own or with others. It is hard work. Spending an hour and a half praying through the church members' list is as tiring as anything I know. But it is as much a part of my work as turning up on time on Sunday morning.

Wonderfully, it is also a source of joy. A commitment to making prayer central in ministry brings joy when it is answered! Think of the story recorded in Acts 12: Peter has got on the wrong side of Herod, who incarcerates him: 'Peter was kept in prison, but the church was earnestly praying to God for him' (Acts 12:5).

God is not going to let the momentum of the word be deflected by a mere tyrant like Herod. So he sends a supernatural agent, an angel, with a speciality in jail breaks. Peter is a bit bemused, but decides in the end that it isn't a dream. He goes round to the house where the church prayer meeting is still going! He knocks. A servant girl called Rhoda answers:

> 'When she recognised Peter's voice, she was so overjoyed she ran back without opening it and exclaimed, "Peter is at the door!"

> "You're out of your mind," they told her. When she kept insisting that it was so, they said, "It must be his angel." But Peter kept on knocking, and when they opened the door and saw him, they were astonished.' Acts 12:14–16

Notice the joy and the astonishment. OK, so this is an unusually spectacular answer to prayer. But every person in Christian ministry knows what it is like to be surprised and overjoyed by prayers being answered. We are part of a supernatural project: the divine word is spreading through this world with powerful momentum. One of the main things that seems to make it slow down is when people in ministry ignore the supernatural dimension of the work and neglect prayer.

It happens to me: I slip into thinking that if I simply study harder and accumulate more knowledge; or if I plan things more meticulously; or if I get other people working even harder, doing things the way I think they should be done, then the momentum will pick up again. In fact, the opposite is true. God has shown me that again and again. In his gentle grace he has brought me to a sense of hollowness when I think I can do it myself and a realisation of failure when all our best efforts include only token prayers. And from the empty feelings of disappointment, I turn to him and say, 'Lord, can you do something about this?', and things change.

I think of a time in Nottingham years ago when our church caretaker and his wife were being harassed by neighbours. The police appeared impotent, so we called a church prayer meeting. The next week the aggressive family was rehoused 50 miles away. I think of a godly Bible scholar affected by kidney disease and about to prepare for a life on dialysis (a dismal prospect) who was pronounced healed by his consultant after a time of prayer with the church elders. I think of the time I longed for money to pay for a student worker, realised I hadn't prayed about it, started praying and found an email offering £100,000 over five years. These are special moments spread over 25 years.

They are the exception: the norm is rather different and even more exciting. It is to pray and pray and pray for people over years and years and see God at work in their lives, bringing the re-creating word into their hearts, nurturing that new creation in their lives so they find more and more rest in Christ, so that they are able to endure what they would have thought unendurable, so that they turn their backs on the attractions that compete with Christ for first place in their hearts, so that they walk on choppy waters of life hand in hand with Christ.

In all that there is extraordinary joy.

That can be your joy too. It really can. All the sacrifice, all the things we give up in order to pray, all the energy expended. All worth it.

Lord, you have taught me so much about prayer over these 20 years in Cambridge. Perhaps more about prayer than almost anything else apart from pain. And the two have gone together. Thank you so much for the pain and frustration and disappointment that has made me pray more. I really mean that, Lord! Because it has led to so many answered prayers. Many of them have been quite small things but they have all reminded me that I am not alone and that living as if you weren't interested is daft. Thank you for times recently when we got a bit concerned about the church finances and you got us praying about it. Both times, things improved. I think most of all of the people I have prayed for and the changes you have brought in their lives: their conversions, their growth, their love, their hope. I could not have made those changes: but you did. I look back and I do wonder why I haven't prayed more: as I look forward, do all you need to do to keep me praying, even if that means hitting road blocks or seeming dead ends or feeling really powerless: I really want you to do those things if you need to keep me praying. Amen.

MINISTRY AND PREACHING

At the heart of ministry is preaching. The momentum of God's loving power, which was released at the cross, has surged through time, turning lives inside out, repairing hearts that were beyond repair, confronting both the dejected and the smug with an irresistible love far better than they have previously found or even dreamed of. And this has always happened through people speaking that word.

God chose to save us through the humiliation of the incarnation of the cross and he chooses to bring that salvation to us through the ludicrously over-optimistic plan of human beings giving talks and having conversations. I wonder sometimes why he doesn't write the words in the sky or make a giant fist appear to knock some sense into us. But preaching (and by that I mean all sorts of ways we communicate the gospel) is his plan. In ways that confound all expectations, it has worked.

And that requires us to be servants of the word. The apostles described their core responsibilities as prayer and the word – specifically, the *service* of the word.

How can we apply that specifically to preaching? It means that preaching is not about me. Not about my fulfilment or my ego. When I am preparing a sermon I am the servant of the word: it is not the servant of my ego or needs. Too often I try to make it that. I can tell. I am ashamed to explain this, but I think I must. I know I am getting this the wrong way round when I finish preaching, go to the door of the building and immediately hope that I will meet certain people who will tell me that the sermon (or some part of it) was accurate, scintillating, helpful or at least acceptable. Sometimes I even find myself manipulating the conversations to try to make them say those things: how truly pathetic, Lord, but you are patient.

Preaching is my serving the word – not the other way round. I want people, above all, to think Christ is great and his word is amazing and to have as few thoughts of me as is possible. But the temptation is always to use preaching (of any kind) as a kind of self-promotion.

I had lunch recently with someone who had been involved in one of the most prominent and successful churches in the United States – until it all went sour. Today the church, which once had more than 10,000 people in it, no longer exists. My lunch companion said he had observed something happening: for many years the founding pastor (who was the main preacher) concentrated on preaching the text of the Bible. But over time, things changed. The sermons were still powerful, but they seemed to derive their authority not from the text of the Bible but from the personal forcefulness and opinions of the preacher. It sounded to me as though he had moved away from being a servant of the word.

To take it a little further, this means that I am not free to impose my agendas on the word. I serve it by communicating what it says, not what I want it to say, and by including parts which I would rather leave out. I find it hard to over-state how important this is – and how the temptation to do otherwise never goes away. It is, I think, greater for me now than it has ever been, because the gap between what seems obvious to modern folk and what the Bible says is broadening all the time.

I had a recent experience of this which rather shook me. I was coming to the end of a long series on Isaiah, 50 sermons in all. In the last section of Isaiah (56 – 66) you find that a number of passages seem to repeat the same themes. That is true of 59:15–20 and 63:1–7.

In both of them the Lord is seen coming as a mighty warrior, bringing judgment and salvation. The second passage is rather lurid: the Lord is pictured with blood-spattered robes, the blood coming from a human winepress where he has been treading down his enemies.

Judgment is a hard thing to preach in our culture. At least I find it hard, and the human winepress seemed a particularly difficult prospect. I had intended to touch on 63:1–6 when I preached on chapter 59 but I never quite got round to it. The programme had me moving straight on from the end of 62 to a new section starting at 63:7. So I was off the hook! I could avoid the blood-spattered clothes completely. What a relief.

Except it wasn't. I felt increasingly uncomfortable skipping over the blood-spattered robes. I didn't even have the excuse that I had to finish the book by the end of June: there was a 'spare' Sunday with no sermon text allocated.

In the end I changed my plans and preached on 63:1–6: not just as part of a longer sermon but as the whole text for that morning, almost the shortest passage I preached on in the whole series.

It was a most powerful morning. I hadn't really got it all sorted in my mind in advance but as I preached, two things that I had always seen as different and even in conflict merged and fused. I found myself preaching that Christ is beautiful not just when he saves but when he judges as well. For him not to judge, not to put things right, would be the most grotesque ugliness. A vision of the beauty of Christ being expressed not just in his saving love but in his righteous judgment hit me for the first time as I preached it. And it felt as though the penny had dropped for others as well. Several confirmed this later. I felt so glad the Lord had got me to the place where I was more scared of failing to serve his word, than of what it might sound like.

Serving the word needs a bit more fleshing out. It means spending lots and lots of time studying and thinking about sermons. At times that is exhausting. It can be particularly demanding for extroverts, people whose batteries are recharged by other people. Most sermon and talk preparation is solitary: it means long hours on our own at a desk or table, reading, puzzling, taking notes, playing with ideas. For an extrovert, that is draining. How much easier to pinch someone else's idea or outline and get on with what energises me more – seeing people!

Let's dwell a little longer on the self-denial that serving the word implies. It is not only working out the original meaning of the passage. That is plenty of work on its own. But it is only half of the preacher's job done. I then have to work out how the claim and promises of this particular text connect with the lives of the people I'll be speaking to. If I don't think this way I will present a scathing denunciation of first-century Pharisees for everyone to enjoy, or a great description of the magnificence of King David, or an intricate unweaving of the complexities of a bit of Paul so that everyone can now see the skeleton under the skin of the passage.

The service of the word calls me to go a lot further: this means knowing people, knowing their lives, their hopes and fears: both generally in our culture and also individually, because in fact I am preaching to people, not types. This takes its own kind of mental effort and creativity.

I'm preparing to preach on John's Gospel later this year. How do the particular themes of John intersect with the Christians in my church and the non-Christians outside my church who might, please God, come and see what we are up to one Sunday? The statement 'In the beginning was the Word' brims with significance: but how does it particularly fulfil the unexpressed longings and emptiness of folk in Cambridge, while correcting their false, limited views of self and life and history?

I can't say everything about it in one sermon and I can't spend sermon after sermon on it. So what should I draw out that will release the energy of the text for these people at this time? The temptation for me is to be lazy, to stick with an explanation of the text in its original setting with a few rather standard suggestions for connections, rehashing what I have heard others do or done myself without much fresh thought. If I am making the word serve me, that is what I will do. If I accept that I am there to serve the word, I can't leave it there. I have to force myself to think a bit more.

Sometimes I go through a couple of dozen sermon outlines until I reach one that I think will most help people. Quite often I reach a point where the passage just seems unreachable (at least by me) and have to go out for a run to seek God. At times I battle with the passage because it doesn't say what I would prefer it to say and I don't want to give in, or because it says far more that I can possibly preach and I haven't a clue what to do with it.

Fortunately I am not alone. When we choose to serve the word, it is not a choice to submit to a depersonalised text, as though I was giving myself to Chairman Mao's *Little Red Book* or Marx's *Das Kapital*. Even there you would be aware of the (dead) author behind the text. But with the God's word, the author is neither dead nor distant. The word never ceases to be the word of God, which means God's speech; and God is present in his speaking.

In all of the labours of preparing to preach, God is there with me: it is up to me how much I recognise and realise this presence and how much I try to operate effectively on my own. For the preacher who is attentive to the presence of God in his word as he prepares, a wonderful discovery awaits. The word speaks to you. He speaks to you. The magnificence of what is being said fills your vision. The word confronts me. I am unmade and remade. It shines into my darkness, and as I receive it with faith I find I am taking new steps as a toddler child of God.

And that holy supernatural presence draws me in love to the people I will be speaking to. Sometimes I find it pushing me to put down a commentary and to pick up our church members' list, open it, look at the photographs and pray for people. Sometimes I have felt on a Saturday night that I can't go to bed without praying for everyone in the membership list as to how they will hear the sermon the next day. That kind of serving the word is pretty demanding and costly: my poor wife has had to learn that Saturday evenings are generally very different to the way they would be if I was in different work.

But all of it is worth it. Worth it in the lives that are rebuilt, in steady little steps, week by week. Worth it for the connection with God it brings me both in preparation and preaching. Worth it for what Martyn Lloyd-Jones called 'the romance of preaching', not knowing quite what God may or may not do in any one sermon and so often finding that although I am such an inadequate messenger, something has taken flight in one person's soul and someone else desperate for a drink has found a cup of cool water in the heat of their lives.

Lord, you helped me through that first sermon and however many more it has been since then. You know that too often I've been less the servant of the word than someone trying to be its master. Is that getting better as I get older? I hope so, Lord. I want to thank you that I've seen the word healing spiritual diseases and making sleepy people zealous for you. It's been the food that has sustained dozens of faithful people in their weekly rhythms of obedience and self-denial. And I've seen your word rescue a church from its confusion and pain and take it to a very different place: not my preaching – your word, in its unstoppable momentum of self-giving love. What a gift, to see that happen. Thank you. It's all from you and about you. Amen.

MINISTRY AND
THE LONG-TERM

By now you are getting the idea, I hope. Ministry means sacrifice, commitment and even pain. but it is worth it. Here is a summary of what that looks like over time from Psalm 126:5–6:

> 'Those who sow with tears
>   will reap with songs of joy.
> Those who go out weeping,
>   carrying seed to sow,
> will return with songs of joy,
>   carrying sheaves with them.'

Like so many biblical writers, he describes God's work in agricultural pictures. That's not really surprising in an agrarian society. We find the same pictures in Jesus' parables, especially the parable of the Sower, which predicts highly variable responses to the sowing of gospel seed. Paul also uses the imagery when he talks about how he planted seed in Corinth and Apollos watered it but God made it grow (1 Corinthians 3).

The psalm writer picks up the hard side of agricultural work. It can be back-breaking. Out in all weathers, your work affected by so many factors beyond your control, needing to be done over and over and over again. Having said that, it is hard to imagine many farmers with tears running down their faces unless the bags of seed are simply too heavy! The picture is of people engaged in God's work, who really do groan under the strain and the pressure – and at times feel like crying because it is hard work and the results are patchy or slow.

You need to realise that this is the normal pattern for the ministry of the word. The word's momentum is unstoppable but it goes at God's pace. Often its work is invisible, like an underground river, full and powerful, but not seen from the surface of the land.

The normal pattern for gospel ministry is regular sowing of the seed of the word, again and again and again. Week after week, year after year. For much of the time the immediate visible results are disappointing for anyone with high expectations. Most of the time, God's work in people's hearts does not jump forward with unusual crisis experiences and huge step changes. Those things happen, praise God. But it is not the normal way. The normal pattern is gradual, like the slow growth of a large tree rather than the way a tropical plant can put on a foot of new shoots overnight. And that is where there is growth! Much of the seed does not even produce lasting plants and fruit.

We have to embrace this reality or we will be disappointed with ourselves, our churches or even with God. It may tempt us to give up, move somewhere

where we think it might be more productive, or to adjust what we are doing in ways that cut bits of the gospel out or compromise God's truth to make him fit in with the culture.

This need to embrace a long-term perspective is especially important for folk in the early years of paid ministry, when expectations are often sky-high and horizons quite short-term. But it also matters for folk who have been in ministry longer who feel disappointed. Some of the time what they need to do is to look with more discerning eyes to see the growth that is really there. But we all also need to hold onto the great promise of an eventual harvest. That promise is repeated by Paul in Galatians 6:7–9:

> '**Do not be deceived: God cannot be mocked. A man reaps what he sows. Whoever sows to please their flesh, from the flesh will reap destruction; whoever sows to please the Spirit, from the Spirit will reap eternal life.** *Let us not become weary in doing good, for at the proper time we will reap a harvest if we do not give up.*' (my italics)

He tells us there is a connection between inputs and outputs: what you sow is what you will reap. At a personal level that means sowing the gospel in your life will one day produce eternal life for you. But he extends it to how we work with other people too:

> 'Therefore, as we have opportunity, let us do good to all people, especially to those who belong to the family of believers.'
> Galatians 6:10

And doing good surely includes all our efforts with people inside and outside the church to sow gospel seeds in their lives. So let's read the promise again:

> 'Let us not become weary in doing good, for at the proper time we will reap a harvest if we do not give up.' Galatians 6:9

He cannot mean that we should not get tired, because that is normal and human. And ministry requires exhausting work or we are not giving ourselves properly. All work is by definition tiring and that includes ministry. The end of the verse explains it – he is talking about the kind of weariness that means we consider giving up, rather than resting and getting back to it. I know what that feels like. It can come when we have been overdoing it and our system just can't face any more and we can't imagine continuing. By the end of an academic year I find my mind sometimes unable to process information properly, as though I was trying to run the same software on an old computer without the right chip speed and memory. At other times, I am just exhausted and feel I don't have any capacity to bear anyone else's needs. Usually a break helps with that.

But there is another kind of weariness in doing good: when we feel that the results are so disappointing that it just isn't worth it. That is different from simple exhaustion, though it is sometimes connected with it. It is an issue of morale. It is a loss of hope. The grind of ministry is worth it if we see or expect results. If we don't see or expect results, we begin to think it just isn't worth the effort. Why bother?

That is why this promise is so important. God guarantees results for gospel work. In the end the harvest will come. That is his promise to you.

How does that work? Sometimes it comes when after years of faithful work first one, then another, then a flurry of folk all come to faith at the same time. Or there is a surge of energy in the life of the church in response to our preaching and people come to life spiritually in a new way.

In my experience that is like a church member whose spiritual life looks like an underground stream, barely more than a trickle, being fed by more and more underground springs and widening into a powerful river until eventually the surface can contain it no longer and it pours out above ground. And those on the surface realise that a huge amount has happened gradually over time under the surface which they had barely noticed.

But there is a further horizon. That is when the full extent of our work is revealed, tested and rewarded at the return of Christ. And that is the subject of the next chapter.

Lord, I just don't get it. I get so fired up about a sermon and it seems to preach really well and then... nothing much. I pray my heart out for sudden, massive, visible effects but it feels just like a stone disappearing into a pond, with a few ripples that gently fade into obscurity. Then I wonder if it is all having any effect. But I've discovered you know what you are doing. Thank you for the people who email years later and say that a sermon really did something in their hearts in that moment. Thank you for the small steady growth in so many people which I can see over years and even decades when I really look. Thank you for the weekly miracles of the word of God by which you keep us walking with you along the narrow way. Thank you for the songs of joy you've got me singing again and again when another bit of the harvest comes home. Amen.

MINISTRY AND HEAVEN

It is hard, working to a distant goal. Most of us live for short-term goals: getting through today, getting through the week to the weekend or day off, getting through the term to the holidays etc.

In ministry we need those short-term horizons. We are human beings and that is only human. But the long-term horizons matter too. And one long-term horizon matters supremely.

The value of our lives will be revealed. Think of an Olympic rower who has been aiming at the Games. For perhaps seven years (or even longer) she has been working towards that moment when she lines up in her country's women's quad boat in the Olympic final. Another analogy is the PhD student who has been studying his subject for so long he has almost forgotten what it was like before he was interested in physics. After a three or four-year period of intense research he has produced a thesis, and at the end of it he has to face his examiners: how will they assess his work? Will it be up to standard?

When Christ returns, lazy Christians and lazy ministry workers are in for a shock. But faithful ones can expect a very special kind of joy.

The parable of the talents, or the bags of gold, is scary for people who don't develop the gifts God has given them. Within the larger structures of grace and salvation, there is a variety in our experience of joy. But for those who use what God has given them, there is this prospect: to be welcomed with the words: 'Well done, good and faithful servant!' (Mt. 25:21).

My 'call to ministry' came through a number of different things at different times. I started preaching, for example, when the minister of our church needed someone to fill in for him by preaching one Sunday evening, and rang me by mistake, having dialled the wrong number! He didn't want to admit it, so he asked me to preach and I did. It was a good sermon, largely because he dictated it to me. Later he invited me to join his church staff.

After a while I began to think that I might have the gifts needed for pastoral ministry, at least in embryonic form. But I also started to realise how much it would cost us – a lower standard of living, lower prestige, lots of pressures and demands. I felt sorely tempted to see out my time in that church and then go back to publishing or even try something else, like becoming a barrister, which I had always fancied. I was aware that lots of our friends seemed to be able to have good and rewarding careers and the joy of roles in church life as volunteers. It was a real battle for me.

Then one evening, I think it was Bonfire Night, though I am not sure of any direct connection, the parable of the talents came rushing uncomfortably into my mind. I imagined meeting Christ after I died and his asking me what I had done with the gifts he had entrusted to me. I knew in a flash that if I had not at least given paid ministry the best possible 'go' I could, I would not be able to look him in the face. And I knew that that would be the worst feeling in the universe. That feeling has never left me. At times when the immediate rewards of ministry have seemed vanishingly thin and its demands on me have felt particularly attritional, that moment has come back and helped me on.

Paul links this explicitly to people.

> 'what is our hope, our joy, or the crown in which we will glory in the presence of our Lord Jesus when he comes? Is it not you? Indeed, you are our glory and joy.' 1 Thessalonians 2:19–20

The effort of ministry now will bring a transcendent joy in heaven. Paul finds this deeply motivating: it is his 'hope.' *They* are his hope. This brings us back to the heart of ministry. It is unlike a PhD, because it is not all about me. It is a bit more like a rowing team because that is a collaboration between people. But the model is more like that of the coach of a sporting team who is given a responsibility for his athletes.

Personally I have experienced such joy in helping people take new steps in ministry and then seeing them grow.

We can also expect pleasant surprises, fruit from our work that we never knew about in this life. Why can I predict that so confidently? So often we only hear about the effect of something we did years afterwards, like the person who we talked to about Christ who became a Christian ten years later. Our part was a small one but significant and indispensable in the story she tells of that journey.

God's word always does it work: Isaiah insists that it simply will not return empty to him (Is. 55:11). So if we don't seem to see much in the way of solid results now, presumably that means that when all is finally revealed, we can expect to find out all sorts of things that have happened. We have a hint of what part of this will look like in the parable of the Sheep and Goats in this exchange:

> "'Then the King will say to those on his right, 'Come, you who are blessed by my Father; take your inheritance, the kingdom prepared for you since the creation of the world. For I was hungry and you gave me something to eat, I was thirsty and you gave me something to drink, I was a stranger and you invited me in, I needed clothes and you clothed me, I was ill and you looked after me, I was in prison and you came to visit me.'

"Then the righteous will answer him, 'Lord, when did we see you hungry and feed you, or thirsty and give you something to drink? When did we see you a stranger and invite you in, or needing clothes and clothe you? When did we see you ill or in prison and go to visit you?'

"The King will reply, 'Truly I tell you, whatever you did for one of the least of these brothers and sisters of mine, you did for me.'" Matthew 25:34–40

That gives us a humble confidence: if we are faithful now, we will, by God's help, have been far more effective than we have ever dreamed.

Lord, thank you that you are not a hard taskmaster. Thank you that you are not unreasonable. Thank you that you give gifts and then help us use them. Thank you that you walk with us. Thank you that you give the reward of more of yourself, more opportunities to serve you. Oh, help me be faithful to my calling. Help me give myself to you and your work. I feel such conflict inside between serving you and living for myself. Keep the vision of your welcome in heaven clearly in my mind. Help me to live for that more than for anything else. Amen.

OUR DEEPEST JOY

We have been emphasising that the spread of the word of the gospel through the world requires lives of service and self-sacrifice from those in ministry. The starting place is not self-fulfilment but self-denial. Yet we have seen in every chapter how that leads to joy. The biblical texts all point to this great outcome even though it is not the main target.

But we need to remember that the main joy we know is not through the successes of ministry but in Christ himself and the salvation he has guaranteed us. In Luke 10, Jesus sends 72 of his disciples out on a short-term mission trip. They come back, faces glowing with excitement. It has been spectacular. They have seen supernatural power flow through them:

> 'The seventy-two returned with joy and said, "Lord, even the demons submit to us in your name."' Luke 10:17

It's so brief that we can miss how ecstatic they were and just what they had been able to do. They had been able to exert authority over dark spiritual forces that had dominated people's lives. Imagine that! I think I would be pretty happy too and I would certainly want to tell Jesus all about it.

His reply is interesting. He validates the experience:

> 'He replied, "I saw Satan fall like lightning from heaven. I have given you authority to trample on snakes and scorpions and to overcome all the power of the enemy; nothing will harm you."' Luke 10:18–19

They were not exaggerating and there was nothing fanciful about their analysis of it. They really were on top of the demons with divine power. Then he feels the need to correct something:

> 'However, do not rejoice that the spirits submit to you, but rejoice that your names are written in heaven.' Luke 10:20

He senses that their reaction to the exorcisms they have been able to perform is not quite right. That is where they are getting their joy from. Something more important has been marginalised. The more important thing is simply this – their salvation. He expresses it in this lovely image of a list in heaven of the people who belong to him. His followers' names are on that list. They can *know* that for certain. They can be *sure* of it. And that is the deepest joy in their lives.

I love ministry and it has brought me all sorts of joy. But I am tempted to make joy in ministry, especially a sense of being gratified when something I have done has turned out well, too important.

What matters most is simply that the eternal love of God has descended into the deep darkness of my soul with the light of his glory. What matters most is that the glory has entered my world and dealt with my sin on the cross. What matters most is that there is a place for me in his new creation. And that the power of that new creation is already at work in me. Nothing can take that away. Even if I never preached another sermon that would still be true and would be enough.

I had a difficult time in 2006 and ended up having five months off work with stress, depression and anxiety. I returned to work after Christmas and my fellow leaders wisely helped me to ease back in. One Sunday morning early on, all I did was the reading. The next week I contributed a prayer. After the service I stood at the door to talk to people as they left.

Everyone was very nice to me. But I began to spot a pattern. They were nice to me, but they were talking to my colleague Marvin differently – thanking him for the sermon (and it was a good one), being grateful that he had visited them that week, getting out diaries to arrange to see him, discussing arrangements, church activities he was currently leading in my place.

I began to feel quite hollow and useless. I was used to the affirmation and the connections. Now Marvin was getting them all and I seemed like a beached whale – still breathing but not swimming, and not much use to anyone. Then I had a little word with myself:

'That's a silly way to respond: you are a son of God: he is your father! That is what gives you your identity, that is where your joy comes from.' Things improved instantly, as a sense of the Fatherly love of God was poured out gently in my heart, and I have tried to gain my joy from that ever since. Because whatever the ups and downs of ministry, our primary identity is not as ministers, nor our primary relationship with those we minister to. Being loved by Christ and having our names written in the book of life are the supreme and growing joy. And nothing can take that away except our own choice to look elsewhere.

Lord, I am so grateful that I'm safe. Safe in you and what you did on the cross for me. I can hardly believe it! My name is in your book. Ministry is full of excitement and life in general is full of happy things. I do find that these other joys become more important to me than you in yourself and for yourself. Thank you that at times you have diluted those other joys or even removed them completely. And in those moments you have been unutterably precious. Amen.

FINALE

I sat down for afternoon tea with the adult son of a friend of mine. Inevitably we turned to talking about his father. I said how much he had meant to me as a teacher, mentor and friend. I asked how he was. His son paused. He thought and he said: 'His 50s were a pretty hard time for my dad. But they didn't sour him, they made him sweeter.'

And it all clicked into place. I had been listening to his father's sermons, some of them preached during those difficult times in his 50s. They were great sermons, better than any I will ever preach: I would love to be able to preach like that. But I had also been listening to some more recent sermons. And they were different.

One way to describe them was the word his son had used: 'sweeter'. There was a new sweetness of love for the people in his church with nothing phoney or contrived about it. Someone once said: 'Sincerity is the key to success. Once you can fake that you've got it made'.

There was nothing fake about my friend's sweetness towards his congregation.

And there was more. Because there was a deeper sweetness about Jesus Christ, without it ever being sentimental or sickly. In his words, you could feel how much he knew about the deep richness of knowing Christ – and that to refuse Christ was not just wrong, it was daft and self-defeating. His love for Christ and for his congregation were really two aspects of the same thing – a new personal depth that had come from a deep encounter with Christ through the hard things in his life, which made him an even more effective and beloved pastor.

I find this encouraging in so many ways and I want you to as well. First and foremost, you can open yourself up to whatever God wants to do to you in ministry and in life. Because he can make it a pathway into sweetness. Whether you take the pathway into sweetness, or the path that goes off the other way into sourness, is your call and you need to open yourself to being given the strength of purpose to go the way my friend went.

If you are thinking of starting out in ministry and worried by the sacrifices and pressures it will mean, don't let that put you off. They will probably be much worse than you expect! But it will be worth it.

If you are in the middle of a life of ministry: look back. What has God done to bring more sweetness into your heart and your work? Perhaps you look back a bit ashamed because it is at best a mixed picture, and perhaps you have let sourness in. It does not have to finish there! Remember the change my friend's son observed in his father between the ages of 55 and 65. You do not have to get stuck! The sourness can be transformed into sweetness if you let Christ's Spirit do a gentle but firm work of showing you more of Christ. The next ten years can be quite different, they really can. And all the sacrifice and suffering will seem all the more worth it, if you let God be God in your life.

When I began, I had no idea what serving the word of God as a pastor would look like. I had a sense that there would be joy because that was what I had seen in my first mentor. But that first brief period of church work was easy and unpressured. What followed my theological training was some six years of turmoil. But that and several difficult times since then have all been worth it.

I took up running in my late 40s. Joining a club raised my expectations of how much faster I could get in races of different lengths. I was inspired by the achievements of others. I was also inspired by the belief of others, in particular one friend called Christof. He describes himself as: 'Left-handed, left-wing, vegetarian, rationalist, scientist, lecturer, programmer and autodidact. Keen cyclist, runner and all-round optimist.' In 2015 he was voted the top lecturer in the Cambridge university medical school. He has his own rather interesting views on athletic training (and much of life) based on evidence rather than received wisdom or dogma.

But to get to the point: Christof believed (and I think believes) in me and my potential as a runner more than I believed (and maybe believe) in myself. The first time I ever met him was running round the Cambridge University Athletics Track. 'So what is your time for a 5km race? 21 minutes? You could go under 20!' He was soon encouraging me to think big about marathon times too.

Not only does he believe that I can run faster than I believe, he also believes I can do the level of training needed to get there. And training basically means suffering!

His belief in both things led me to levels of training in 2015 that I would have thought quite impossible. And I reaped the reward, with much faster times at 5km and marathon distances. The 5km improvement was so good people thought I should be tested for drug use. The marathon improvement was even more satisfying because that challenge is so much more extreme.

But here is the thing. For both of those races, Christof did not just inspire me to train much harder than I thought I could. Or raise the bar for me to aim at a time much faster than I thought I could. He *paced* me round both races. That means that he ran with me from start to finish, checking my time (and even my heart rate), slowing me down or speeding me up gently, and above all, encouraging me constantly.

'Great running, Julian.' 'Julian, you are running like a sub-3hr marathon runner.' 'Julian, who do you want to beat? Your brother-in-law's best time? You can do it.' 'Julian, I can feel awesome levels of awesomeness coming on you.' That last one is real, and verbatim. If it sounds cheesy, all I can say is that it was exactly the kind of cheese I needed at about mile 18 when my hips felt as though they had been injected with red-hot metal.

After the marathon I wrote a rather pretentious race report which I posted on the club website[4] and I finished it like this:

My wife misread a post-race text and thought I had written that Christ had helped me round (that's another dimension I won't go into here save to say *Chariots of Fire*): well, Christof isn't quite in his league, but as a marathon coach and pacer, there are little resemblances to someone rather greater and I am very grateful to both.

In the end, my running is trivial, only significant as it points to greater things. But the greater thing is this: the living presence of Jesus Christ in the life of the Christian minister. He believes you can be sweeter than you think. He believes you can be more resilient than you think you can. He believes that you can be holier and more loving than you think you can. And he believes much more than you do that you can endure the hardship, the suffering, the repeatedly chosen acts of service, the extreme pressures of ministry and life.

And he will be there, pacing you through. You cannot possibly do it alone. But you do not have to do it alone. He will stick by you. During that marathon the wind was blowing hard. When we were running into it, Christof insisted that I ran behind him so he could shelter me. Christ does the same.

When I met Christof at a race, he asked me what my time had been. 'That's all very well,' he said. 'But now you need to get down to some serious training.' What he meant was more rigorous, more demanding, more painful than I could imagine. But it led to the improved race times I have been boasting about for the last few paragraphs, paced by him.

I wonder what Christ might be saying to you? And to me. What recommitments to serving him in ministry? What new areas of self-denial or patient endurance? Will we become servants of the word, not to achieve personal joy, but in the hope that our service will be joyful? Will we embrace the sacrifice it means? Will we submit to the trials, and the people, God sends into our lives to break us so that he can make us something more beautiful than we were or could have been any other way? Will we give ourselves to the work and the people, ready to wait for results and recognition, happy to do it strong in faith that the word has an unstoppable momentum from the death and resurrection of Christ? Will we let him take us forward into the challenge of ministry, confident that he will be with us every step of the way and that in him it can be a joy?

Lord, reading that, what else can I do but say 'Yes'? 'Yes' to your love and your work. 'Yes' to being a servant of Christ and his word. There is no other way to find myself, no other way to get any kind of purchase on this mysterious life in time and body, with all my confusion and conflictedness about what it means to be me. Even here, Lord, I sound as though you were there to help me find myself. The truth is that I say yes to you and I still don't fully understand myself. I still don't know why I seem to have more instinctive love to give people on some days than others. If I say yes to you to try to find myself as an independent whole being in this life, I think you just laugh and let me find a bit more darkness in my soul, yet another grim, cold, murky, pulsing zone that I can neither overcome nor understand. But I look again to you and I say yes to you and in that I find rest and renewed vigour to serve. Because in Christ I am whole and safe and united with the word that is advancing so powerfully. And as I say yes to you, I realise that may mean that you need to break me all over again: well, Lord, that's fine. I want more than almost anything else for the next decade and a half (or however long you want me to be at Eden) to make me sweeter, not sourer. Whatever it takes. Bring it on, Lord. For what has been, thank you. For what will be, your will be done. Whatever it may be. Because in Christ it will bring glory and joy. Amen.

NOTES

1. Balthasar, Hans Urs von, The Glory of the Lord VII. *Theology: the New Covenant* (Bloomsbury Academic, 1990) p.113

2. I got this powerful phrase from my friend in ministry, Steve Midgley, via one of his curates.

3. Ray Ortlund Jr, blogpost on Isaiah 57:15.

4. http://runcambridge.org.uk/news.cgi?item1=201511 with the heading *Eight times round an airfield*. Warning: it is a bit long and if it were shorter would qualify for Pseuds' Corner in *Private Eye*.

MORE IN THIS SERIES

ON BEING A SERVANT OF GOD
Warren Wiersbe
978-1-910587-10-2

THE CALL
Trevor Archer & Paul Mallard
978-1-910587-50-8

WHY FREE CHURCH MINISTRY?
Graham Beynon
978-1-910587-49-2

TO FLY TO SERVE
Adrian Reynolds
978-1-910587-60-7

a division of **10** of those.com

10Publishing is the publishing house of **10ofThose**. It is committed to producing quality Christian resources that are biblical and accessible.

www.10ofthose.com is our online retail arm selling thousands of quality books at discounted prices.

For information contact: **sales@10ofthose.com** or check out our website: **www.10ofthose.com**